2025 Calendar

January

MO	TU	WE	TH	FR	SA	SU
		1	2	3	4	5
6	7	8	9	10	11	12
13	14	15	16	17	18	19
20	21	22	23	24	25	26
27	28	29	30	31		

Fabruary

MO	TU	WE	TH	FR	SA	SU
					1	2
3	4	5	6	7	8	9
10	11	12	13	14	15	16
17	18	19	20	21	22	23
24	25	26	27	28		

March

MO	TU	WE	TH	FR	SA	SU
					1	2
3	4	5	6	7	8	9
10	11	12	13	14	15	16
17	18	19	20	21	22	23
24	25	26	27	28	29	30
31						

April

MO	TU	WE	TH	FR	SA	SU
	1	2	3	4	5	6
7	8	9	10	11	12	13
14	15	16	17	18	19	20
21	22	23	24	25	26	27
28	29	30				

May

MO	TU	WE	TH	FR	SA	SU
			1	2	3	4
5	6	7	8	9	10	11
12	13	14	15	16	17	18
19	20	21	22	23	24	25
26	27	28	29	30	31	

June

MO	TU	WE	TH	FR	SA	SU
						1
2	3	4	5	6	7	8
9	10	11	12	13	14	15
16	17	18	19	20	21	22
23	24	25	26	27	28	29
30						

July

MO	TU	WE	TH	FR	SA	SU
	1	2	3	4	5	6
7	8	9	10	11	12	13
14	15	16	17	18	19	20
21	22	23	24	25	26	27
28	29	30	31			

August

MO	TU	WE	TH	FR	SA	SU
				1	2	3
4	5	6	7	8	9	10
11	12	13	14	15	16	17
18	19	20	21	22	23	24
25	26	27	28	29	30	31

September

MO	TU	WE	TH	FR	SA	SU
1	2	3	4	5	6	7
8	9	10	11	12	13	14
15	16	17	18	19	20	21
22	23	24	25	26	27	28
29	30					

October

MO	TU	WE	TH	FR	SA	SU
		1	2	3	4	5
6	7	8	9	10	11	12
13	14	15	16	17	18	19
20	21	22	23	24	25	26
27	28	29	30	31		

November

MO	TU	WE	TH	FR	SA	SU
					1	2
3	4	5	6	7	8	9
10	11	12	13	14	15	16
17	18	19	20	21	22	23
24	25	26	27	28	29	30

December

MO	TU	WE	TH	FR	SA	SU
1	2	3	4	5	6	7
8	9	10	11	12	13	14
15	16	17	18	19	20	21
22	23	24	25	26	27	28
29	30	31				

Contact List

Name ______________________
Handphone ______________________
E-mail ______________________
Notes ______________________

Name ______________________
Handphone ______________________
E-mail ______________________
Notes ______________________

Name ______________________
Handphone ______________________
E-mail ______________________
Notes ______________________

Name ______________________
Handphone ______________________
E-mail ______________________
Notes ______________________

Name ______________________
Handphone ______________________
E-mail ______________________
Notes ______________________

Name ______________________
Handphone ______________________
E-mail ______________________
Notes ______________________

Name ______________________
Handphone ______________________
E-mail ______________________
Notes ______________________

Name ______________________
Handphone ______________________
E-mail ______________________
Notes ______________________

Name ______________________
Handphone ______________________
E-mail ______________________
Notes ______________________

Name ______________________
Handphone ______________________
E-mail ______________________
Notes ______________________

Contact List

Name _______________________

Handphone _______________________

E-mail _______________________

Notes _______________________

Name _______________________

Handphone _______________________

E-mail _______________________

Notes _______________________

Name _______________________

Handphone _______________________

E-mail _______________________

Notes _______________________

Name _______________________

Handphone _______________________

E-mail _______________________

Notes _______________________

Name _______________________

Handphone _______________________

E-mail _______________________

Notes _______________________

Name _______________________

Handphone _______________________

E-mail _______________________

Notes _______________________

Name _______________________

Handphone _______________________

E-mail _______________________

Notes _______________________

Name _______________________

Handphone _______________________

E-mail _______________________

Notes _______________________

Name _______________________

Handphone _______________________

E-mail _______________________

Notes _______________________

Name _______________________

Handphone _______________________

E-mail _______________________

Notes _______________________

Contact List

Name ___________	Name ___________
Handphone ___________	Handphone ___________
E-mail ___________	E-mail ___________
Notes ___________	Notes ___________

Name ___________	Name ___________
Handphone ___________	Handphone ___________
E-mail ___________	E-mail ___________
Notes ___________	Notes ___________

Name ___________	Name ___________
Handphone ___________	Handphone ___________
E-mail ___________	E-mail ___________
Notes ___________	Notes ___________

Name ___________	Name ___________
Handphone ___________	Handphone ___________
E-mail ___________	E-mail ___________
Notes ___________	Notes ___________

Name ___________	Name ___________
Handphone ___________	Handphone ___________
E-mail ___________	E-mail ___________
Notes ___________	Notes ___________

Password Tracker

Website	Website
Username	Username
Password	Password

Website	Website
Username	Username
Password	Password

Website	Website
Username	Username
Password	Password

Website	Website
Username	Username
Password	Password

Website	Website
Username	Username
Password	Password

Website	Website
Username	Username
Password	Password

Password Tracker

Website	Website
Username	Username
Password	Password
Website	Website
Username	Username
Password	Password
Website	Website
Username	Username
Password	Password
Website	Website
Username	Username
Password	Password
Website	Website
Username	Username
Password	Password
Website	Website
Username	Username
Password	Password

YEAR AT A GLANCE

YEAR: _________________

JANURARY

- ☐ _______________
- ☐ _______________
- ☐ _______________
- ☐ _______________
- ☐ _______________
- ☐ _______________
- ☐ _______________

FEBRURY

- ☐ _______________
- ☐ _______________
- ☐ _______________
- ☐ _______________
- ☐ _______________
- ☐ _______________
- ☐ _______________

MARCH

- ☐ _______________
- ☐ _______________
- ☐ _______________
- ☐ _______________
- ☐ _______________
- ☐ _______________
- ☐ _______________

APRIL

- ☐ _______________
- ☐ _______________
- ☐ _______________
- ☐ _______________
- ☐ _______________
- ☐ _______________
- ☐ _______________

MAY

- ☐ _______________
- ☐ _______________
- ☐ _______________
- ☐ _______________
- ☐ _______________
- ☐ _______________
- ☐ _______________

JUNE

- ☐ _______________
- ☐ _______________
- ☐ _______________
- ☐ _______________
- ☐ _______________
- ☐ _______________
- ☐ _______________

JULY

- ☐ _______________
- ☐ _______________
- ☐ _______________
- ☐ _______________
- ☐ _______________
- ☐ _______________
- ☐ _______________

AUGUST

- ☐ _______________
- ☐ _______________
- ☐ _______________
- ☐ _______________
- ☐ _______________
- ☐ _______________
- ☐ _______________

SEPTEMBER

- ☐ _______________
- ☐ _______________
- ☐ _______________
- ☐ _______________
- ☐ _______________
- ☐ _______________
- ☐ _______________

OCTOBER

- ☐ _______________
- ☐ _______________
- ☐ _______________
- ☐ _______________
- ☐ _______________
- ☐ _______________
- ☐ _______________

NOVEMBER

- ☐ _______________
- ☐ _______________
- ☐ _______________
- ☐ _______________
- ☐ _______________
- ☐ _______________
- ☐ _______________

DECEMBER

- ☐ _______________
- ☐ _______________
- ☐ _______________
- ☐ _______________
- ☐ _______________
- ☐ _______________
- ☐ _______________

WEEKLY PLANNER

PRIORITIES

TO-DO

Notes

Monday

Tuesday

Wednesday

Thursday

Friday

Saturday

Sunday

2025
JANUARY

Monday	Tuesday	Wednesday	Thursday	Friday	Saturday	Saturday
		1	2	3	4	5
6	7	8	9	10	11	12
13	14	15	16	17	18	19
20	21	22	23	24	25	26
27	28	29	30	31		

REMINDER

NOTES

2025
FEBRUARY

Monday	Tuesday	Wednesday	Thursday	Friday	Saturday	Saturday
					1	2
3	4	5	6	7	8	9
10	11	12	13	14	15	16
17	18	19	20	21	22	23
24	25	26	27	28		

REMINDER

NOTES

2025
MARCH

Monday	Tuesday	Wednesday	Thursday	Friday	Saturday	Saturday
	1	2	3	4	5	6
7	8	9	10	11	12	13
14	15	16	17	18	19	20
21	22	23	24	25	26	27
28	29	30				

REMINDER

NOTES

2025
APRIL

Monday	Tuesday	Wednesday	Thursday	Friday	Saturday	Saturday
	1	2	3	4	5	6
7	8	9	10	11	12	13
14	15	16	17	18	19	20
21	22	23	24	25	26	27
28	29	30				

REMINDER

NOTES

2025
MAY

Monday	Tuesday	Wednesday	Thursday	Friday	Saturday	Saturday
			1	2	3	4
5	6	7	8	9	10	11
12	13	14	15	16	17	18
19	20	21	22	23	24	25
26	27	28	29	30	31	

REMINDER

NOTES

2025

JUNE

Monday	Tuesday	Wednesday	Thursday	Friday	Saturday	Saturday
30						1
2	3	4	5	6	7	8
9	10	11	12	13	14	15
16	17	18	19	20	21	22
23	24	25	26	27	28	29

REMINDER

NOTES

2025
JULY

Monday	Tuesday	Wednesday	Thursday	Friday	Saturday	Saturday
	1	2	3	4	5	6
7	8	9	10	11	12	13
14	15	16	17	18	19	20
21	22	23	24	25	26	27
28	29	30	31			

REMINDER

NOTES

2025
AUGUST

Monday	Tuesday	Wednesday	Thursday	Friday	Saturday	Saturday
				1	2	3
4	5	6	7	8	9	10
11	12	13	14	15	16	17
18	19	20	21	22	23	24
25	26	27	28	29	30	31

REMINDER

NOTES

2025
SEPTEMBER

Monday	Tuesday	Wednesday	Thursday	Friday	Saturday	Saturday
1	2	3	4	5	6	7
8	9	10	11	12	13	14
15	16	17	18	19	20	21
22	23	24	25	26	27	28
29	30					

REMINDER

NOTES

2025
OCTOBER

Monday	Tuesday	Wednesday	Thursday	Friday	Saturday	Saturday
		1	2	3	4	5
6	7	8	9	10	11	12
13	14	15	16	17	18	19
20	21	22	23	24	25	26
27	28	29	30	31		

REMINDER	NOTES

2025
NOVEMBER

Monday	Tuesday	Wednesday	Thursday	Friday	Saturday	Saturday
					1	2
3	4	5	6	7	8	9
10	11	12	13	14	15	16
17	18	19	20	21	22	23
24	25	26	27	28	29	30

REMINDER

NOTES

2025
DECEMBER

Monday	Tuesday	Wednesday	Thursday	Friday	Saturday	Saturday
1	2	3	4	5	6	7
8	9	10	11	12	13	14
15	16	17	18	19	20	21
22	23	24	25	26	27	28
29	30	31				

REMINDER

NOTES

BUSINESS OVERVIEW

YEAR ________________

MY BUSINESS SUMMARY

BUSINESS NAME

SOCIAL MEDIA HANDLES

- INSTAGRAM
- TIKTOK
- FACEBOOK
- PINTEREST
- YOUTUBE
- OTHER

BUSINESS DETAILS

- WEBSITE
- LAUNCH DATE
- OWNER
- PHONE
- EMAIL
- LOCATION

GOODS AND SERVICES

SUMMARY OF MISSION

BUSINESS OVERVIEW

YEAR _____________

FUNDAMENTAL IDEAS

MISSION AND VISION?

TARGET MARKET?

PRODUCTS/SERVICES?

REVENUE MODEL?

COMPETITORS?

SWOT ANALYSIS?

Order Form

Date :   Order # :

Product:

Description:

Company / Website:

Email:

Phone:

Notes

Item #	Description	Quantity	Price	Amount

Shipping Details	Subtotal

Ship Date:

Shipping Company:

Tracking Number:

Notes

Discount:

Tax:

Shipping:

Grand Total:

SWOT ANALYSIS

Determine your company's internal strengths and weaknesses using a SWOT analysis. Then, take advantage of outside chances for strategic growth while reducing risks. Updating it frequently aids in adapting to shifting market conditions.

STRENGTHS

WEAKNESSES

OPPORTUNITIES

THREATS

Competitor Analysis

Identify Competitor

Competitor	
Product/Service	
USP	

Competitor Strategies

Which Are Some Important Tactics Employed by My Competitors?

How Can I Set Myself Apart? How Can I Improve?

MARKETING PLAN

Channel	Marketing Tactics	One-time Fee	Monthly Cost
Total Cost:			

Business Intelligence

HOW CAN WE IMPROVE CUSTOMER EXPERIENCE?

WHAT NEW PRODUCTS OR SERVICES CAN WE OFFER?

HOW CAN WE MAKE OUR BUSINESS MORE SUSTAINABLE?

HOW CAN WE LEVERAGE DIGITAL TRANSFORMATION?

MARKETING PLAN

HOW CAN WE DIFFERENTIATE OUR PRODUCT IN THE MARKET?

WHO IS OUR TARGET MARKET FOR THIS PRODUCT?

WHAT FEATURES WILL MAKE OUR PRODUCT STAND OUT?

WHICH MARKETING CHANNELS WILL BEST PROMOTE OUR PRODUCT?

Collection Ideas

Product Type:	Digital:	Physical:

PRODUCT NAME/DESCRIPTION	RELEASE DATE

Product Analysis

HOW DOES OUR PRODUCT COMPARE TO COMPETITORS?

WHAT FEEDBACK ARE WE RECEIVING FROM CUSTOMERS?

1. HOW IS THE PRODUCT PERFORMING AGAINST KEY METRICS?

PRODUCT PRICING

PRODUCT PRICING CALCULATOR

HOURS PAID:

AMOUNTS MADE EACH HOUR :

MATERIALS COST PER UNIT:

COST OF MATERIALS PER UNIT :

OTHERS PER UNIT, POWER BILLS, ETC.:

ALL OF THE ABOVE COMBINED TOTAL UNIT COST

PRODUCT MARKUP FOR 30% PUT 1.3 ETC

ENTIRE PRODUCT COST ALL-IN-CLUSIVE COST & MARKUP

MODES OF RECEIVING PAYMENT:

LAUNCH YOUR SHOP

This checklist addresses everything from the fundamentals of business and strategy to the more hands-on elements of actually opening your store. It has every essential component you'll require to start and grow a lucrative online storefront.

- [ ] **CHOOSE A BUSINESS NAME**
- [ ] **DECIDE ON PRODUCTS**
- [ ] **FIND A SUPPLIER**
- [ ] **SET A BUDGET**
- [ ] **REGISTER YOUR BUSINESS**
- [ ] **SET UP YOUR SHOP PLATFORM**
- [ ] **DESIGN A LOGO**
- [ ] **TAKE PRODUCT PHOTOS**
- [ ] **SET PRICES**
- [ ] **CREATE PRODUCT LISTINGS**
- [ ] **SET UP PAYMENT METHODS**
- [ ] **DECIDE ON SHIPPING**
- [ ] **SET RETURN POLICY**
- [ ] **CREATE SOCIAL MEDIA ACCOUNTS**
- [ ] **TELL FRIENDS AND FAMILY**
- [ ] **LAUNCH THE SHOP**
- [ ] **MONITOR ORDERS**

WEBSITE PLANNER

WEBSITE NAME:

LOGIN:

EMAIL:

PASSWORD:

GOALS OF THE WEBSITE:

INSTALLED PLUGS

THEME SETUP

PERSONAL INFO

KEY LINKS

NOTES

PRICE LIST

PRODUCT NAME	SKU ID	PRICE

CUSTOMER RECEIPT

<table>
<tr><td>RECEIPT NO:</td><td>DATE:</td></tr>
<tr><td>ITEMS:</td><td>AMOUNT:</td></tr>
</table>

THANK YOU FOR YOUR PURCHASE!

<table>
<tr><td>RECEIPT NO:</td><td>DATE:</td></tr>
<tr><td>ITEMS:</td><td>AMOUNT:</td></tr>
</table>

THANK YOU FOR YOUR PURCHASE!

<table>
<tr><td>RECEIPT NO:</td><td>DATE:</td></tr>
<tr><td>ITEMS:</td><td>AMOUNT:</td></tr>
</table>

THANK YOU FOR YOUR PURCHASE!

<table>
<tr><td>RECEIPT NO:</td><td>DATE:</td></tr>
<tr><td>ITEMS:</td><td>AMOUNT:</td></tr>
</table>

THANK YOU FOR YOUR PURCHASE!

<table>
<tr><td>RECEIPT NO:</td><td>DATE:</td></tr>
<tr><td>ITEMS:</td><td>AMOUNT:</td></tr>
</table>

THANK YOU FOR YOUR PURCHASE!

<table>
<tr><td>RECEIPT NO:</td><td>DATE:</td></tr>
<tr><td>ITEMS:</td><td>AMOUNT:</td></tr>
</table>

THANK YOU FOR YOUR PURCHASE!

Customer Feedback

PRODUCT	FEEDBACK

Order Tracker

DATE	ORDER #	QUANTITY	CUSTOMER	DONE
				◯
				◯
				◯
				◯
				◯
				◯
				◯
				◯
				◯
				◯
				◯
				◯
				◯
				◯
				◯
				◯
				◯
				◯
				◯
				◯
				◯
				◯
				◯
				◯
				◯
				◯
				◯
				◯
				◯
				◯
				◯
				◯

Tax Deduction

DATE	CATEGORY	EXPENSE	AMOUNT

Monthly budget Planner

Income

Date	Description	Amount
Total		

Fixed Expenses

Date	Description	Amount
Total		

Other Expenses

Date	Description	Amount
Total		

Bills

Date	Description	Amount
Total		

NOTES

SUMMARY

AMOUNT

INCOME	
BITS & FIXED EXPENSES	
VORABLE EXPENSES	
DEBT	
BALANCE	

Long Term Business Goals

Long-term business goals focus on sustained growth, profitability, and market expansion. These goals help shape the company's direction for success over several years.

1 YEAR GOALS	5 YEAR GOALS

Steps to Take Action	Steps to Take Action

10 YEAR GOALS	15 YEAR GOALS

Steps to Take Action	Steps to Take Action

Annual Finance

YEAR: _______________

MONTH	INCOME	COSTS	BILLS	SAVINGS	DEBT
JANUARY					
FEBRUARY					
MARCH					
APRIL					
MAY					
JUNE					
JULY					
AUGUST					
SEPTEMBER					
OCTOBER					
NOVEMBER					
DECEMBER					
TOTAL					

NOTE

Annual Profit & Loss

YEAR: ______________

Product	Sale Price	Cost	Fees	Shipping	Profit	Loss

Meeting Notes

DATE AND TIME:

NEXT MEETING DATE:

ATTENDEES

DISCUSSION POINTS

AGENDA ITEMS

ACTION ITEMS

Marketing Plan

CHANNEL	BUSINESS METHODS	ONE TIME COST	MONTHLY COST
Facebook			
Instagram			
LinkedIn			
Twitter			
TikTok			
Mailchimp			
Sendinblue			
ConvertKit			
Google			
Bing			
Google Ads			
Bing Ads			
Medium			
WordPress			
YouTube			
Vimeo			
Amazon Associates			
ShareASale			
Upfluence			

SEASONAL PROMOTIONS

YEAR: _______________

JANURARY

- ☐ _______________
- ☐ _______________
- ☐ _______________
- ☐ _______________
- ☐ _______________
- ☐ _______________
- ☐ _______________

FEBRURY

- ☐ _______________
- ☐ _______________
- ☐ _______________
- ☐ _______________
- ☐ _______________
- ☐ _______________
- ☐ _______________

MARCH

- ☐ _______________
- ☐ _______________
- ☐ _______________
- ☐ _______________
- ☐ _______________
- ☐ _______________
- ☐ _______________

APRIL

- ☐ _______________
- ☐ _______________
- ☐ _______________
- ☐ _______________
- ☐ _______________
- ☐ _______________
- ☐ _______________

MAY

- ☐ _______________
- ☐ _______________
- ☐ _______________
- ☐ _______________
- ☐ _______________
- ☐ _______________
- ☐ _______________

JUNE

- ☐ _______________
- ☐ _______________
- ☐ _______________
- ☐ _______________
- ☐ _______________
- ☐ _______________
- ☐ _______________

JULY

- ☐ _______________
- ☐ _______________
- ☐ _______________
- ☐ _______________
- ☐ _______________
- ☐ _______________
- ☐ _______________

AUGUST

- ☐ _______________
- ☐ _______________
- ☐ _______________
- ☐ _______________
- ☐ _______________
- ☐ _______________
- ☐ _______________

SEPTEMBER

- ☐ _______________
- ☐ _______________
- ☐ _______________
- ☐ _______________
- ☐ _______________
- ☐ _______________
- ☐ _______________

OCTOBER

- ☐ _______________
- ☐ _______________
- ☐ _______________
- ☐ _______________
- ☐ _______________
- ☐ _______________

NOVEMBER

- ☐ _______________
- ☐ _______________
- ☐ _______________
- ☐ _______________
- ☐ _______________
- ☐ _______________

DECEMBER

- ☐ _______________
- ☐ _______________
- ☐ _______________
- ☐ _______________
- ☐ _______________
- ☐ _______________

Monthly Sales

COMPANY	MONTH	YEAR

Day	Orders	Products sold	Top-selling item	Daily income

ADVERTISING TRACKER

PRODUCT	STAGE	START DATE	END DATE	COST

EXPENSE TRACKER

DATE	CLASSIFICATION	SYNOPSIS	AMOUNT	BALANCE

INCOME TRACKER

DATE	CLASSIFICATION	SYNOPSIS	AMOUNT	BALANCE

SALES TRACKER

DATE	PRODUCT	ORDER NO.	QTY.	PRICE-COST= PROFIT

COST & PROFIT TRACKER

DATE	PRODUCT	PRICE	COST +FEES + SHIPPING	PROFIT

LOSS & PROFIT TRACKER

DATE	PRODUCT	PROFIT	LOSS	EVALUATION

PURCHASE TRACKER

DATE ORDER PLACED	PRODUCT	STORE	QTY.	DATE RECEIVED

INVENTORY TRACKER

DATE	CATEGORY	DESCRIPTION	AMOUNT	PRICE

Coupons & Discounts

DATE	END DATE	COUPON CODE	DISCOUNT	USED	PRICE

Bill Payment Tracker

DATE	DESCRIPTION	BILL	AMOUNT

Return Tracker

DATE	ORDER	CUSTOMER	REASON FOR RETURN	TRACKING #

Suppliers List

PRODUCT	DESCRIPTION	WEBSITE	COMPANY	EMAIL

Return Tracker

DATE	ORDER	CUSTOMER	METHOD	TRACKING#	FEE

NOTES